Mary B Wetmore

Sounds from Home and Echoes of a Kingdom

Mary B Wetmore

Sounds from Home and Echoes of a Kingdom

ISBN/EAN: 9783337183851

Printed in Europe, USA, Canada, Australia, Japan

Cover: Foto ©ninafisch / pixelio.de

More available books at **www.hansebooks.com**

SOUNDS FROM HOME
AND
ECHOES OF A KINGDOM.

BY
MARY B. WETMORE.

CINCINNATI, OHIO.
THE EDITOR PUBLISHING COMPANY.
1898.

CONTENTS.

Introduction	9
Echoes of a Kingdom	15
First Letter	18
Second Letter	24
Third Letter	27
Fourth Letter	30
Fifth Letter	35
Sixth Letter	43
Seventh Letter	46
Eighth Letter	58
Ninth Letter	70
Tenth Letter	74
History of Kaahumanu	94
Twelfth Letter	97
Thirteenth Letter	105
Greeting to the Provisional Government	118
Plants and Shrubs	120
Fruits	121
Coffee	122
Ferns	123
Organ Recital	124

SOUNDS FROM HOME.

LAU-PA HOE-HOE.

SOUNDS FROM HOME.

INTRODUCTION.

"Home" is an old-fashioned word, so is Gungle's "Song without Words;" neither of them obsolete, however, for which we are truly thankful.

"Home, Sweet Home," with its memories, its

partings, its home-comings, are ties cherished alike in the palace of the king and the cot of the peasant.

In days of yore, as now, there were musical gatherings, musical evenings, in which the artist and amateur joined alike. There were the talented Russian violinist and the ever encouraging kindly artist with his beloved violoncello, the enthusiastic student, the amateur, and when the classic *concerto* or *sonate* was finished someone would unconsciously drift into the lighter vein of Gungle's melody, until each instrument became involved in the dreamy *andante* strains.

Only once does the music grow frivolous and gay; then quickly lapses into the sedate measure and resumes its wonted dignity; nothing to be jolly about after all.

We are to listen to the echoes from Hawaii, and cannot linger over home matters; there are goodbyes to say, a trunk to pack.

It is just as well not to ask too many questions; as, How far away is the sunny land? Is there a cable? etc., etc., it might produce discomfort; just hie yourself away, and leave all the cold and the snow behind you, and revel a while in a tropical clime.

Therefore, in the afternoon of a day in early winter when the autumn breezes were kindly lingering and the chilling blasts were gathering for their winter carnival, the traveler departed for that land of sunshine, that little kingdom over the sea, Hawaii.

Again we wander among home sounds and memories concerning a party of musical friends who hoped to lose sight of earthly cares and troubles, such as partings and farewells, in the music of the glorious chorals and numbers of Handel's Oratorio of the Messiah.

We are seated in the opera house; on the stage we see the familiar faces of the many members of the chorus of the "Detroit Musical Society," with their leader, Mr. Frederick Abel, at the baton; below is the waiting orchestra; it is a fair scene; the blazing crown of lights, the brilliant crowded house, the tints of the pretty gowns with the palms and ferns for a framing. As recitative, solo, and chorus followed in turn, the air seemed filled with requiems; there was the sympathetic voice of the soprano whom—— had hoped to hear in that wonderful anthem, "I know that my Redeemer liveth;" and there were actually tears in the beautiful voice of the contralto when she sang the solo, "He was despised and rejected." Then came the soul-reviving "Hallelujah chorus," and soon they were home again, living as it were in the dim religious light of a cathedral, with nothing to do, but a prayer to say; and outside those chilling blasts were keeping their word, holding high carnival. Eolian harps, tubas, trombones, with an occasional piccolo, were executing a Wagnerian *finale* for homers.

A memory also, of a merry little lad who sent a "Sound from home," all done up in a queer little missive that went spinning across the sea to the traveler, bearing some wonderful signature, understood doubtless by the recipient, it may have been Hawaiian, or Indian in its characters; nevertheless, this was how the correspondence began over that Peaceful (?) Sea, under whose waters were no lines to flash the message for weal or woe from shore to shore; must wait for the letter delayed, possibly by such little episodes as from the heart of the Islands comes the word, "Mail Carrier treed by wild cattle, will not reach steamer in time."

Thus ends our little prelude to the strains from other lands; and like as the traveler departed for distant lands, thus do these portions of home letters in journal fashion go forth encircled with home surroundings and musical memories or " Sounds from Home."

ECHOES OF A KINGDOM.

"Land of the West! beneath the heavens
There's not a fairer, lovelier clime,
Nor one to which was ever given
A destiny more high, sublime."

As a trip over the continent has been so often written up, it will be scarcely worth while to jot down the journal-like letters descriptive of this part of the journey. One pervading thought, however, tinged every impression during the ride by rail, viz: wonder and admiration of the beauty of the West. How narrow are our views, we who seem to look only to an Eastern boundary. How wonderful.

"Those palaces of nature, those vast walls,
That pinnacle in clouds their snowy scalps."

The deep canons, miniature Niagaras, those rolling prairies, the mines of gold and silver, the glittering jewels brought to earth's surface. In the far West the fair girl, the belle of some

Eastern city, casts willingly her future with the ambitious college graduate, and all the cosmopolitan grace and polish that one could wish for greet you as you linger for awhile in some Western town. In pleasant contrast also comes the stop for a few minutes at some ranch settlement where a swarthy face and stalwart form in the picturesque costume of the cowboy expresses your idea immediately of all that you imagined. The warm shake of the hand from the undaunted farmer who, through hardships equal to those of the pilgrim fathers, has come out of the conflict for bread and butter fairly well. He tells you all about it as he drops into the seat beside you in the car.

To vary that experience comes an invitation to dine or sup with some titled rancher who understands how to live at the foot of the Rocky Mountains, or elsewhere, on the ranch, or otherwise, entertains also after a manner and hospitality that tell a story of baronial inheritance and ancestral home, and all deserted for the freedom of this western life in America.

As we near an occasional army post we call to mind every move registered in the army journal, and are tempted to linger.

In each and every garrison must be surely "some one we used to know," it may be the hero of some Indian battle field, or perhaps the last year's graduate of West Point, one of the soldiers of the future, newly domiciled.

Kind hearted people everywhere; life and death, human wants and wishes, joy and sorrow, seem to make the whole world kin. By way of counterbalance, however, to all this make-up of goodness, the glimpse at one station of two or three manacled train robbers of Christmas Eve fame was certainly very satisfactory and interesting.

Here we are at the Golden Gate, all prefaces ended; and on January 31st, 1888, the staunch steamship, "Australia," bears the traveler across the sea to the land of sunshine and waving palm.

ECHOES OF A KINGDOM.

"The proud Pacific chafes her strand
She hears the dark Atlantic roar."

Honolulu, Feb. 9th, 1888.

My last word to you was from shipboard just before leaving San Francisco, at the hour of 2 P. M. the 31st of January. The weather was very rough from the Golden Gate. Smooth water was promised us after going over the bar; but it did not come until the Islands were reached. The ship rolled and plunged wildly, and I must say that those who enjoy storms at sea may have them; I have had enough.

The storm, we learned, was the result of what was called the "Kona," at the Islands, a species of hurricane which has not visited them for six years. I am keeping up with the general style of our trip by having exceptional weather; the captain had not experienced so rough a trip since he had been on the route, and during the storm it was very agreeable to hear the quiet tread of the quartermaster across the deck, and the bell striking the hour. After meals there is a gathering of the smokers in the smoking room, which I enjoy very much. Some of the officers in true sailor style, tell their yarns and stories very interestingly.

We have some great travelers aboard ship; among them a Mr. Alexander, of Honolulu, a veritable "globe trotter," a sugar planter also, and sending last year eight thousand tons of raw sugar to the San Francisco market.

There are twenty-four Chinese aboard as stokers, coal heavers, etc., who make excellent hands, doing their work well, and what is peculiar, I have not seen one of them with a grimy face. Almost any other native would come on deck with begrimed face; but the chief engineer tells me that they each have their pail of water and bathe and change their clothes before coming on deck.

I forgot to mention that on the stormy night the main boom broke loose and fell with a thundering crash on the deck just over our heads.

Life on shipboard became rather monotonous, and I rejoiced when on Wednesday morning about five o'clock on looking out of my window, a soft air blowing, Cocoanut Island and Diamond Head of Oahu loomed up on the starboard bow and the harbor of Honolulu was in sight. Earth, sky and ocean in such marvelous coloring mentioned by some poet as, "A dainty picture in green and gold, the work by a master hand." I felt as if I had reached my Mecca, the land of everything beautiful; but alas for human hopes, what means this small boat wending its way shipward with pilot and health officers aboard!

The "Mariposa" was quarantined on a former trip on account of there being small-pox in San Francisco, and we were not at all sure what reception we might meet with and were extremely anxious. They came on board, the yellow flag was run up, inspection began, and greatly to our disgust the bulletin read that passengers would be allowed to procure cottages on shore and pay the expense of a government guard. Ship passengers to be quarantined for eighteen days from date of leaving San Francisco, making ten days more before we could be free.

For all of this, I suppose we must thank the President of the Board of Health. The ship reached the dock; cargo was unloaded by

Kanaka longshoremen and custom house officers; others came and went, but not a soul was allowed to leave the ship without permission of the Board of Health, until a place was secured where we could be under guard. Two or three of our passengers, residents of Honolulu, not allowed to go to their homes, rented a vacant house near their own residences.

Twelve of us interviewed the proprietor of the Hawaiian Hotel, and it was arranged that he was to procure a cottage for us where we could be guarded for ten days. We remained aboard ship all day and took our final dinner with the captain, who also were not allowed to go ashore, and at six o'clock, in carriages, the devoted twelve having agreed to lodge together, were driven to the house from which I am now writing.

Allow me to give you an idea of our quarantine abode: The hotel, a very pretty and picturesque structure, has for its grounds a large square, and in this square belonging to the hotel are the cottages, and the entire grounds are filled with tropical trees, plants and flowers. With these at our summer resorts the sight would indeed be novel and wonderful, with us it is an every day picture. The house is a two story one with porches above and below; very comfortable rooms were assigned us. In front of the house is a high iron fence and stone post; the hall wide, and runs through the house from front to rear. I am now writing in the hall and as I look out the doorway one could almost imagine it a large greenhouse, only no greenhouse at home could possibly show the same wealth of plants, etc. I asked the doctor (who has all the names at his tongue's end) to make a list of the varieties. On each side of the front porch is a tall palm tree and beautiful flowers are all about us. I was awakened last night by the strange notes of birds that I never heard before. I caught some of them and have reduced them to writing.

A clarionette would give you this bird's call as I note it down.

Our meals are sent over from the hotel and we have a Chinese attendant at our table in the hall. In front of the house inside of the iron gates stands our guard; our boundary is limited by a line marked twenty feet from the gate. If a friend of one of the party calls, the visiting must be done at a distance of twenty feet. I shall endeavor to pass the hours of the days of the quarantine in writing letters, reading, smoking, and watching the passers-by, the latter forming a kaleidoscope well worth seeing. As one of the evidences that we are in another clime, one of our party was awakened last night by the sting of some insect, and found on examination that he had been bitten by a centipede; the bite is harmless, however. There are no tarantulas or snakes here.

ECHOES OF A KINGDOM.

QUARTERS OF AUSTRALIAN QUARANTINE CLUB,

DUDOIT COTTAGE, HONOLULU, Sunday, Feb. 12, '88.

Still in quarantine, and expect to be for some days shut up and guarded. It is a queer sensation to be a prisoner and sit by the hour on the veranda of the cottage and see strange faces and people flock by on their way to church. To see the church (English) thus (which is a handsome one of stone, just a block off) and yet not be able to step out of the gate, or even be allowed to go near it, seems very strange. This is becoming wearisome in spite of the pleasant and beautiful things and charming weather about us. I can step off the porch and pick a banana, orange or mango, but I would prefer to step outside the gate. The guard sits or lounges about in front, and visitors shout their messages at twenty feet away.

We pass the time pleasantly, however; we

write a little, smoke, and then take our walks about the house, trying a few military tactics by way of exercise. The weather is simply superb. This being Sunday, the street panorama is peculiar. The Chinese are out in force; it is their New Year; the gay ones seem to delight in riding horseback, and gallop madly up and down the street, while groups of Chinese women and children pass by. They are most beautifully dressed; I saw one family where there were three little girls, miniature Chinese, about six years old,. with flowers adorning their heads. Their dresses are of fine material and beautiful colors. The din of firecrackers is constant. Dr. McGrew called at the gate today. Dr. Emerson, president of the Board of Health, also called to inspect us today.

By this time the latter is aware that we do not take very kindly to our imprisonment. We assembled after dinner tonight, and the guard finding some songs and hymn books, we tried to sing, all of which did not prove to be a very great success; therefore we gave it up and sat down to read. We have been trying to wear thin clothes here, but so far have not been able to do so. There is a fresh briskness about the air that is quite remarkable, the thermometer ranges from 68° to 76°, not varying very much night or day. The Hawaiian band gave a concert last night, and His Majesty, King Kalakaua, went off on the steamer to Hawaii yesterday. I hope to go to church for evening service this week, (five more days in quarantine.) On Sunday they have Low Church at 9:30 and High Church at 11 o'clock. I have had many delightful conversations with our quarantine party.

ECHOES OF A KINGDOM.

February 16th.

Memorable vine clad cottage, this "cottage by the sea;" all things seem "so near and yet so far." I hasten to write a few lines assuring you that all goes well. Four passengers who were sent elsewhere are with us; among them are Mr. Alexander, and Major Elliot, of U. S. S. "Vandalia," therefore we number sixteen. Although we are situated so pleasantly we find our imprisonment rather irksome; we long for liberty. Climate is simply superb, we live out-of-doors and have good appetites, but feel the want of exercise in our close quarters. The band is played near us in Emma Park, for several evenings past they have played delightfully. On Sunday evening last the Kanaka chorus sang; they have most melodious voices and their language is musical.

"*Aloha*" is used as a greeting or farewell; also as a term expressing affection, as *Aloha œ*, Love to you. *Aloha œ Nui*, signifies, My best love to you.

Last evening several gentlemen of our party gathered on the veranda, and it was curious and entertaining to hear the talk and stories of foreign lands, shipwrecks and whaling voyages, as matters of every day life. They spoke of China, Japan, South America, Iceland, the Caribbean Sea and other places. No talk of New York, Chicago, etc.; apparently they did not exist.

We overlook a yard containing numbers of little wire summer houses containing magpies and various birds. On the fence back of our house is a monkey that is very funny with his antics. Many school children, girls and boys, go by with their books, most of them barefooted, but all clean and neat. You become quite accustomed here to the sight of women going about barefooted, wearing their Mother Hubbard fashion dresses, and being a wet day, lifting this apparently one article of dress, necessarily making an exhibition of ankles that would look very curious in any other land than this. When we leave here we shall very probably go to the hotel, and very likely our entire party will go to the volcano together later on.

If we are out of quarantine I shall go to church at five today. I have learned from the purser today that there was a case of small-pox on board our ship. No one else seems to know of it and I have not mentioned the fact. Everybody was vaccinated on ship-board. There is not a case of small-pox on the Island, but they are terribly afraid of it, and the Kanaka with the first symptom gives up and lies down to die.

Dr. Andrews is busy this morning painting some flower that is rare. The day is warm and I am sitting by the open window. Everybody loafing about. Reading matter has become pretty well exhausted and we are quite ready to go outside and stretch our limbs and enjoy our freedom. I shall probably meet the King before I go away. They say he likes a good game of poker, but as I do not play, I won't be able to take a hand. I notice by the paper that the Queen had a "tea party" and a very "enjoyable time." The policemen here carry no clubs. Dress in white trousers and blue sack coat and white caps. One of them parades past our house and has a sharp eye on every one who stops.

P. S. Messenger from Board of Health is just in with our release; everybody happy; all preparing to move out.

ECHOES OF A KINGDOM.

> An enchanted isle with its splendor gleams
> From Nuuanu to Waikiki,
> From the Pali's heights, historic, grand,
> To the shore of the shining sea!

Honolulu, Feb. 18, 1888.

Sent two letters by sail today. I can scarcely give you an idea of Honolulu and surroundings. You can imagine a beautiful summer resort like our own near town, only ten times more enjoyable, and then try to imagine the foliage. All is green and luxuriant. To drive through tropical groves for hours, full of palms and tropical foliage with flowers on every side, and among all this the pretty little cottages and homes abundant, and always summer, is a picture hardly describable. I cannot with my pen give you any idea of it. The interior of the choicest greenhouse might give you a faint idea. Perpetual summer; in fact, any resort that we know of is insignificant compared to the climate and life here.

Mr. Alexander speaks the Kanaka language quite fluently. We drove with him today and saw all the beautiful places about here, visited also the Mausoleum of the Kings: a chapel of gray granite, windows of stained glass, where lie in state the kings of the last century; watched the Kanakas making *poi*; this is the native food. The sea and mountains are all about us, and if the people in the East, where the cold weather abounds, could appreciate all this wonder of climate on this "Beautiful Isle of the Sea," they would name it "The Garden of the World."

The governor's levee last evening was a brilliant affair; I was presented to Queen Kapiolani and the princess. The former is rather stout, and of course in hue and complexion dark; her dress decollete; endeavored to converse with her, and after saying all the nice things I could think of her chamberlain told me that she spoke no English. This, I believe, is not so, but she speaks the native language as a matter of dignity.

Enquired for letters, of Bishop and Company this morning; they tell me that probably my letters have been sent on to Hilo, as a very important resident of Hilo bears my name; hope to see the native "Hula-Hula" dance this week, and do not know when we will go to the volcano, probably not for several weeks. Dr. McGrew has a fine painting of the wonderful crater of Kilauea; leave in a few minutes to take the stage for Waikiki.

Since writing the above rode by stage to Punahon: such beauty of nature I have not seen before; passed numberless cottages, driving for an hour through a wealth of tropical foliage; now and then a white picket fence covered with a magnificent hibiscus. We passed Chinese and children, and Kanakas riding horses; bunches of flowers and peacock feathers on their heads. The whole country about us was like a perpetual picnic, with the hills and the extinct volcano in the background, from 3,000 to 8,000 feet high, and on the other hand the broad Pacific stretching away to the horizon; I cannot describe it. It cannot be sketched, nor taken into a painting, but I cannot but think if these were only within the reach of the people from the States, it is my opinion that no place under the sun could equal this as a health resort; thermometer varying from 65° to 78°, no enervation in the air. It can well be called the "Paradise of the Pacific."

I told you of attending five o'clock service

KAPIOLANI.

Sunday, yesterday and the day before, and in addition to occupying the King's pew, I made use of his prayer book. The foot-stool was embroidered with "E ka haku e aloha mai." I shall send some photos of the people, etc.

I mentioned having been presented to Queen Kapiolani. In the corner of the room where she sat the other evening were tall staffs with a bunch of silk feathers at the top, called "kohela," emblem of royalty. The women all have very good figures, carry themselves well, and are usually barefooted, and I have written you of their mode of dress.

Lunched today with Mr. Bishop at the club. Honolulu citizens are very hospitable. I understand from the collector of customs that a mail goes tomorrow by sail. Dr. Andrews was born in the Hawaiian Islands. His father was one of the missionaries here fifty years ago, consequently he meets many friends. We propose to purchase horses and make the Island of Oahu on horseback, and think it would be very enjoyable. In this way we can take our time and see more.

Was presented also to Mrs. Judd, wife of the Chief Justice, at the Governor's levee. Tomorrow

(Sunday) I shall try to take in all the churches —Chinese, Kanakas, and all; walked past our old quarantine cottage today. Passengers from the " Zelandia " are there now.

The streets are narrow; sidewalks also. People walk anywhere, street or sidewalk. Stores are small and served by half-caste and Chinese clerks. Chinese are very prevalent here; all house servants are Chinese.

ECHOES OF A KINGDOM.

>The soft trade winds
>Unfurled my country's flag,
>Where waved the palm
>And dusky minstrels sang.

HAWAIIAN HOTEL, HONOLULU, Feb. 22, '88.

Aloha! Loyal to my country and loyal to my home, I seat myself to write how pleasantly I have spent the time for the past few days. Attended 9:30 services (called "first congregation.") This is the mission, with choir of eight Kanaka boys in surplices; after which I passed out into the large yard filled with beautiful trees and found the people gathered for the second congregation, at 11:15. This is the regular parish and made up of English and Germans; no Kanakas; and I stood looking at the queer sights, Chinese families, children, and all so beautifully dressed in rich fabrics, the Sisters of Charity in charge of the school and the orphans, the Kanaka men and women, the half-breeds, the stone church and the palace and the shade of the beautiful trees.

The Bishop in his cassock and knee-breeches crossed the yard to the school; stopped to bid me welcome; had noticed me in the church as a stranger, probably. After a pleasant chat with him of several minutes, he gave me the translation of the text on the foot-stool of the king's pew in church. It is "Lord have mercy (or love) towards me," (literal translation.) I went into church again to hear the regular service. Rev. Mr. Wallace, a fine looking man with good voice and manner, conducted a service just like ours. Very simple. The choir consisted of a chorus of men and women, and there were some very good voices. A different organist played; played very well on an organ of twenty stops.

After dinner, while smoking at the hotel with my friends, Mr. Wallace came over to see me. I found him very pleasant and jolly. He was formerly of Milwaukee, Wisconsin. He knew Bishops Armitage and Worthington, and Doctor Brown; also many others. We had a very pleasant visit and in the evening visited the old Kanaka church; a church built of stone and concrete. No organ but a large Kanaka choir. I was struck with the sweetness of their voices and curious music, and, by the way, yesterday found some books of music and sent them by mail. One of the doctor's missionary friends called for him and took him to drive.

Doctor Noyes and I were smoking and lounging under the trees in the yard of the hotel when Mr. C. R. Bishop, the banker, drove up in his carriage and invited us to drive. We visited the Kamehameha home for boys, the Emma Hospital and the Lunalilo home for old men, and a more picturesque and beautiful sight I do not expect to see than those landscapes on the way, the beauty of which you can scarcely imagine. The mountains and ocean, the endless number of lovely cottages with large and well-kept grounds, and as I have told you before, the wealth of beautiful foliage and flowers that I cannot give you any idea of. Doors and windows all open; verandas everywhere, a sort of universal daily picnic. The people seem to act as if constantly at a summer resort, general air of a pleasant time. Riding on horseback, driving in carriages. Kanaka men mounted on sorry looking nags, wearing wreaths of flowers in their hats; summer aspect over all.

There is an interesting story concerning Mrs. Bishop, wife of the well-known resident here; a native of royal descent, she was sought in marriage by King Kamehameha V at the same time Mr. Bishop was courting her. She refused the king, who would have made her a queen, and married Mr. Bishop; she was a very charitable and noble woman. At King Kamehameha's death he was still unmarried, and retaining his love and admiration for her, sent for her and offered her the succession to the throne, which she refused, and the king refusing to name a successor, the next king was elected; viz., King Lunalilo, whose reign was a short one. When Mrs. Bishop died, a few years ago, she left a large amount of property to the Kamehameha schools; one for boys and one for girls. The first is now running. Mr. Bishop has the disposition of the funds for the second. I learned much of its history from a gentleman whom I accompanied to a meeting of the Social Science Club, held at Mr. Castle's on Monday evening. This is a club made up of the brains of the town, where they discuss topics of science, etc., and I think it would be hard to find a party of twenty-four men better informed on high literature and more cultivated than I saw there.

NATIVES EATING POL.

An opportunity offered for a very pleasant conversation with the Judge of the Supreme Court, Judge Judd. I met his wife, you remember, at the Governor's levee.

The President of Oahu college invited Dr. A. and myself to go out yesterday and stay at the college for a week. Dr. A. accepted, but I declined, having another engagement. Yesterday morning was occupied in looking for books in the native language. Received calls from some of our old quarantine friends yesterday afternoon, who are staying at Waikiki. Received also an invitation from Mr. Castle to dine with himself and family. Mr. Castle is one of the oldest white residents, a charming host and gentleman. They live in a very pretty cottage.

One of the staple articles of food here is a root called taro. It resembles somewhat a sweet potato, and is cooked in various ways. The interior is of a grayish color, and is served regularly on the table as potatoes are with us. The people are very fond of it. The great native dish made from this is called "poi." In one of our rides we saw the place where the Chinese were taking it out of the inside of the taro plant, mixing it with water and putting it in a long trough. The makers sit at each end of the trough, and have a large iron pestle with which they beat the mixture for hours until it is a gray looking mass the consistency of jelly. It is then put in barrels and allowed to ferment. The natives eat it from a bowl, by dipping in their forefinger and carrying it to their mouths. It is served generally in sauce plates with sugar sprinkled over it, and eaten with spoons.

After dinner we sat on the veranda and smoked and talked, (think of this, on February 22nd.) as the band came up to the hotel grounds; I then remembered the morning paper stated they were to play for the U. S. Minister. We had noticed him at the table the day before: he occupies one of the cottages on the grounds near the hotel. I lighted my cigar and strolled over to the grounds; found the U. S. Minister, Mr. Merrill, and his wife seated on the veranda and the band of thirty-three pieces drawn up in front with their stands and music. There was also a large flower bed with a flagstaff in the centre, from which floated my country's flag in the soft trade wind.

Seated in a large easy chair for an hour or

more I listened to the most charming band music. Members of the band were all fine looking natives; they had a magnificent set of silver instruments, and the leader told me that these young band members had all been picked up by him and taught in five years. They receive a regular salary from the treasury, and Mr. Berger is a fine leader. They were so pleased with my enthusiasm that they gave me two of their native choruses with accompaniment of four saxophones, effective and charming. The voices were very sweet and in perfect tune, and the songs were very peculiar. Their *pot pourris* were excellent, and I became very tender-hearted as I heard the soft melodies of "Robin Adair" and "Auld Lang Syne."

When the serenade ended Mr. Merrill gave each boy a good cigar and a bottle of beer, and invited us into the house for a bottle of wine. I ventured a few remarks, all of which were well received. All this happened on the 22nd of February, with a soft warm air blowing, filled with the fragrance of flowers, doors and windows open, where a white duck suit and straw hat seems the proper thing. I suppose you were ringing for your factotum just now to throw on more coal in that exasperating furnace.

I will interrupt my letter to get ready to go out to the U. S. S. "Vandalia." The officers give a reception today and we have invitations. I had intended taking the steamer to Waikiki for a sea bath, but the concert, etc., have made me late, so I will, perhaps, go up to-night and bathe by moonlight.

U. S. MEN-OF-WAR,——HONOLULU HARBOR.

ECHOES OF A KINGDOM.

February 24th, 1888.

Noticing by the paper this morning that a mail goes by sail tomorrow, I must finish this and send it on its way. I went, as I told you, out to the flag ship "Vandalia" on the 22nd. Boats manned by the sailors came to the pier to convey the guests out to the ship. Once aboard the "Vandalia," we were taken in charge by the officers and royally entertained. It was indeed a fine sight, this beautiful harbor with its ships of different countries at anchor, colors flying, stationed here and there.

Aboard the "Vandalia" the guns had been removed aft, everything covered with bunting and canvas and the decks were strewn with some sort of material to prevent slipping. The Hawaiian band furnished the music, and there were officers in sufficient numbers from the two ships to give the ladies of the party all the dancing they cared for. Not wishing to dance,

I enjoyed very much chatting with those I knew while taking in the novel sight around me. The "Vandalia" carries two hundred and sixty men; they gathered in groups forward looking on, and all very jolly; among the officers aboard I met Major Elliot, who was a member of our quarantine. Met also Captain Dyer, of the U. S. S. "Marion," also Captain Schoonmaker, of the "Vandalia." Thus ended the charming and novel experience. The next day took the 9:30 stage for Waikiki, a beautiful beach, the noted bathing resort; charming Waikiki, where one can bathe for hours without chill, or watch the natives apparently in their native element swimming, diving or floating on the undulating long lazy swell of the ocean. Here I took my first ocean bath; after bathing I spent the afternoon watching the Kanakas in the water and walking about the little town; saw some picturesque cottages and grounds; certainly one can lead an ideal life here. Returned home in the evening by stage; found the band playing near the hotel grounds, a pretty sight. Ladies and gentlemen on horseback; many of the ladies ride astride, wearing trousers or divided skirts; this does not seem strange here; one becomes accustomed to curious sights and scenes, and I now pay little attention to customs or fashions that seemed very odd to me at first. I missed my opportunity of seeing the Hula dance, but I send by mail photos which will probably give you an idea of it; one card contains view of palace with King and Queen in the foreground watching the dancers; quite a festive scene; the Queen dressed in "Holoku," or Mother Hubbard fashion. Shades of departed dreams of well dressed women; could one ever endure the sight of a Mother Hubbard, were it donned even by a queen in all her glory? Aloha.

ECHOES OF A KINGDOM.

HONOLULU, Friday, Feb. 29th, 1888.

Once more seated in the writing room of the hotel to tell of our goings and comings. I do not remember exactly where I left off in my last one, but think the last date was the 24th. On that day went up to the college, where we procured horses for our ride around the Island of Oahu. Went for a ride up the Manoa Valley, and dined with the students. As there was a piano, Mrs. H. played for me two of Chopin's Nocturnes, and then by special request played Gottschalk's "Last Hope," my favorite.

On our ride to charming Manoa Valley, picked limes by the wayside; a very delightful ride altogether, but was very lame when I dismounted after a ten mile ride. The president of the college accompanied us; the horses belonged to the boys attending school. They ride to the college, and tying a tethering rope to the horses' necks, let them run loose. The man is very poor here who has not a horse in his dooryard. They do not build barns or stables; a shed is the best they have, and a large majority none at all.

I visited the home of Rev. Dr. H., one of the teachers of the mission school, a fine looking gray-haired man, and there found a meeting of the "Cousins' Society," the descendants of the missionaries, where papers and letters were read by the members; not as interesting to me, however, as to the doctor; he being a descendant of the missionaries, enjoyed it very much. A number of native boys sang their native chorus. We returned home by moonlight.

On Sunday afternoon last I took a carriage and went to see Mr. Berger, the band master. Found him seated at table with coffee and cigars after dinner. Mr. Berger showed me some new pieces he had arranged for his boys to sing, and promised I should have them before leaving for home.

Last night we had the most severe storm of thunder and lightning that has been known here for fifteen years; fifteen inches of rain fell in less than forty-eight hours. Called on the American Minister during the storm; waited for a cessation, and finally had to almost swim back to my quarters. Some of our party took steamer this morning for the volcano. On account of the storm we will postpone our tour on horseback over the Island until Friday.

Visited the government building today and received full information as to our ride over the Island. The steamer Belgic was sighted, and knowing there would be mail for us, delayed starting until the mail had been brought ashore, fumigated, etc. I received my mail, and our horses and trappings were made ready. By the way, they would make a sorry sight on —— Avenue, as they are undersized and ungroomed, with big Mexican saddles, our necessary luggage in rolls of oil cloth tied on before and behind with leather strings. We wore big spurs. My horse was brown, with long tail, not unlike a horse the cowboys ride, and every horse always has a long rope coiled around his neck. I lashed mine to the saddle bow with the strings. The name of my nag was "Topsy," and Dr. A's, "Snip." A fine riding-horse such as you see at home could not be guided or ridden where we ventured, nor could possibly have done the work of these animals.

It was some time before I could learn to ride

my horse easily, although I am a good horseman. There is but one rein used and a heavy curb bit, and the rein is never used except to press against the side of the neck. I at first naturally pulled the rein to stop a gallop. The result was a break-up that nearly threw me over his head. You balance yourself on the saddle and use the spurs. Before the trip was ended, however, I managed everything very well. We started Friday about three o'clock and stopped at Bishop & Company's for the mail, and I put my letters in my pocket for leisure reading when we should stop for the night.

Our afternoon ride was only about eleven miles to Ewa, where we found our host; his wife is the daughter of a native chief named Ie and inherits from her father a large number of acres of land, which her husband is improving and which makes him very rich. The property lies along the Pearl River, which, as you may have noticed, has been granted to the United States for a coaling station. Their house, a pretty cottage, is hidden in a grove of trees. We had a supper of fish, taro, poi, and native oysters. I make a pretense of liking these things; I do not, however, but manage to make a good meal with coffee, bread, meat and rice.

After a comfortable rest and smoke we were shown to our room which was one of the straw houses detached, the side and roof of straw fastened to bamboo; no walls inside. Pegs stuck into the bamboo to hang our clothes on. Mats on the floor. It was clean and neat. I would on no account sleep in one of the real native huts.

We mounted our horses before breakfast and rode over to the rice fields, and to the artesian well which he is boring. They have fine water in this section. After breakfast we packed up and made a start, our host and his wife accompanying us. She was dressed in a dark waist and skirt with trousers strapped down, and rode aside. It was as much as we could do to keep up, as we were a little lamed after a gallop of three miles over the grassy hills. They left us at the big gulch. We rode down into it, and they sat on their horses on the bluff above, watching us, until they looked to us as small as children and their horses the size of sheep. A wild, rocky ride for ten miles up and down among the mountains, and then we found a place for lunch, procured water from a trickling stream and took out a can of potted ham and some hard tack, of which our meal consisted. We unsaddled the horses and tethered them to a tree with fifty feet of rope. Here we rested for an hour or so, then mounted and rode on. The scenery changed as we approached the plateau on the other side of the islands on top of the mountain; here we were on a vast plain stretching out in all directions for miles.

The soft trade winds from the Pacific blowing gently, and our horses galloping, not a soul in sight; few cattle or any animals seen. About three P. M. we came to the edge where a descent begins and we could see the blue ocean stretching away in the distance and the surf breaking on the shore miles before us, the white houses of Waialua just discernible among the foliage.

About four o'clock we drew up at the cottage of Mrs. Emerson. She lives here with her son, who is a bachelor. She is eighty-two years old, the widow of Rev. John S. Emerson, one of the first missionaries. They made us welcome, and we remained here until Wednesday. Sunday I attended church, where service was held

by a native preacher. Of course, it was all
Kanaka, but I could follow it in a translated
edition. After the sermon the presiding deacon
went to the table and the people were called
upon for their monthly contribution. I walked
up and laid down my piece of coin and felt
myself entitled to a seat. The people were all
natives or half white. Not over fifty in the
church, where once thousands attended. The
choir was made up of about six young women
and about as many young men. The hymns,
were on pages 287, 161, and 121, and I think
they used the same book I mailed. After
church the people held a meeting to discuss
whether they should accept the resignation of
Rev. Tunnalao. He has a daughter who is a
leper, and he wished to go with her to Molokai
to care for her. They refused to accept it; but
I understand he went the next day. The following day we rode over to a sugar plantation.
I witnessed the whole process from the cutting
of the cane in the field to the wheeling in big
crates with six oxen to the mill, the crushing of
the cane, the passing of the juice through the
the various pans and boilers, and finally watched
the falling of the granulated mass into the pans;

when properly boiled the mass is turned off in tubs, carried to the centrifugals, (a tank with perforated sides revolving very rapidly,) the molasses forced through the sides and the sugar, of a light brown color, dried and thrown into a bin for bagging and shipping, all done within three or four hours. It was indeed very interesting. The rice fields have to be kept under water, and all this irrigating and work is done by the Chinese.

The fields of rice are very picturesque as the Chinese work them. The different coloring of the fields and the queer straw hats they wear make them look like the little Chinese pictures we see very often. They are very patient and industrious. They get two crops a year off the land. The natives do more in cultivating taro, the native food. This is a large leaved plant and requires to be under water also. You see native men black as negroes working in the black mud among the taro plants, and you meet ponies on the road loaded with it jogging from one place to another without a driver or anybody with them.

At Waialua we passed a few very pleasant days, and started Wednesday morning in company with Dr. M., a young physician, along the beach. Mountains on one side and the sea on the other. Remains of old stone houses and fences all along the route. We turned off at one point and rode into a stone enclosure to see the fish god, a rough stone idol. The road lay along the coast and we found the quicksands at Waimea all safe. They are very dangerous at times. About ten miles we managed to climb into a glen with rock on both sides to partake of our lunch. There was a river here and two native women were hunting for native oysters around the abutments of the bridge, and little naked children were tumbling in the black mud. The elder of the women came up to us and as near as we could make out, wanted us to go over to her house. The younger one also approached us. Neither one was over-dressed. Did not accept, however; we were due at Makeo, where we were to spend the night on a ranch, the owner of which has been on the island for about thirty years. He married a native wife and has thirteen children. I found she could not speak English. She did not appear at supper, but we saw her at breakfast. The children are fine looking young men and girls, mulatto color. Have four daughters married to white men.

Although lame from our ride, we awakened rested and refreshed. Rode up a little valley or glen in the mountains and saw the lair of the hog god. The way these native horses would climb great hills over big stones, and ford streams all full of great boulders, was truly wonderful. At first I could not help being a little nervous as to what would happen if the horse should fall; but they do not fall. They would step carefully from one stone to another, sometimes a leg would slip down and you would think you were gone, but they know better than the riders themselves. They climb up banks that a man could scarcely scale.

We left Lane ranch on Thursday morning and reached the other side of the Pali mountain about two o'clock, and rather than stay so near home at a sugar plantation, decided to climb the historic Pali and come through; and such a climb! On the other side was Honolulu. The road is steeper than a pair of stairs and paved with boulders, large and small. It is about a mile from top to bottom, and after having ridden about twenty-five miles, we were repaid by the magnificent view. We were some time climbing it. I felt sorry for my horse; it was hard work and I am pretty heavy, so I dismounted and led him a little way; I wanted to stop and rest him; and thus we finally reached the top. The road is about eighteen feet in width in some places, and in others narrower, a precipitous cliff at the side; at the top, you look off into the ocean and see on each side ranges of mountains; the sight is indeed glorious from the heights of historic Pali, a battle ground of a Kamehameha.

From this point we rode down the beautiful valley of Nuuano into town, which is as charming and fine a ride as can be imagined, with the harbor of Honolulu before you and a smooth level road, high foliage-covered hills, through a valley of tropical trees, arriving at the hotel at 5:30, feeling well and none the worse for wear; in fact I could have ridden twenty miles farther, a tough looking individual, however; nevertheless on arriving at hotel, our friends came out and envied us the sun-burned hands and faces and the "cowboy" look they accused me of. We felt very heroic and superior; we had ridden around the island on horse-back. Thus ended a ride that in my opinion cannot be equaled in the world in variety of scenery and interesting features; a panorama of hills and valleys, gulches, grottoes, glens, grassy plains, beach and blue ocean. We shall go to Hawaii Monday and make the volcano trip; our friends made the trip in a rain storm, could not wait for the weather to clear. The crater of Kilauea is one of the grandest sights in the world, therefore could not be missed through stress of weather; we may stop off at Hilo and take horses for the volcano trip; we are undecided, however. There is a mail in next week, but we shall be away and it will be forwarded to us at Hilo, Hawaii.

ECHOES OF A KINGDOM.

HAWAII NEI.

Hawaii nei—isles where the Muses dwell!
Isles where Parnassian whispers ever tell
There's sweetest music in thy ev'ry mood;
'Tis voiced in lava field and tangled wood,
On dreary plain, each peak of stony mail,
In crater's pit, each shy, retreating vale.

WAIMEA, HAWAII, March 15th, 1888.

We are in the heart of Hawaii, and where I sit the lofty peaks of Mauna-loa and Mauna-kea are in full view, fourteen thousand feet high, within 1800 feet of the highest Alps; this Island is traversed by other ranges, which give to the coast a most picturesque appearance. As I write, however, the tips, and far down the sides of the mountains are obscured by clouds. I wrote you on our return from horseback ride around Oahu; I mentioned band concerts at the hotel grounds, etc. That same evening Mr. Y. called on me; he was formerly organist in St. John's Church. He is choir master of St. Andrew's Cathedral. Lunched at the club with

NUANUU VALLEY.

Rev. Mr. Wallace, Mr. Paty and others. Spent the rest of the day very quietly; also a very pleasant evening with Captain Dyer, of the U. S. S. "Marion," and Captain Kempf, of the U. S. S. "Adams."

On Sunday I mailed the music of Berger's "Aloha œ," a very simple thing like all the pieces they sing, but it is very melodious as sung by a chorus of twenty-five natives. That night I went to Mr. Castle's for tea, one of the missionary residents who is very polite and hospitable to strangers. On Monday we prepared for our trip to Hawaii, and at three o'clock went to the steamer "Kinau," a very fine little steamer lighted by electricity, with all the modern improvements. The scene at the dock, as we stood on the upper deck waiting, was very picturesque. The natives are very simple hearted. The custom seems to be to decorate departing friends with what they call "leis" (lays.) They are long bands or wreaths, made sometimes of feathers or shells, but generally green leaves or flowers. These are hung from the neck or wound around hats. The one hundred or more dark faces, the many colored "lays," the crying men, women and children embracing and walking about hand in hand was very curious, and it was a novel sight. One couple attracted my particular attention. The man evidently was taking his departure. His straw hat was loaded with "lays" of flowers, and several more hung around his neck. The woman, dressed in the usual gay-colored "holuku (native Mother Hubbard) and the usual flat brimmed straw hat, stood in the midst of the crowd crying and wiping her eyes with a not over-clean handkerchief, their arms around each other, once in a while kissing each other, the sympathizing crowd of friends standing about. Again some one else would go up and kiss him, and all look sorrowful, and nobody seemed to think it strange. They kept up the parting until the gang plank was drawn in, then both came on board the steamer; the woman, a large black native, stepped ashore again, and standing on the edge of the dock began what seemed to be the final parting. He handed her a cigarette, she struck a match, lighted it and took a few puffs and then handed it back to him, and as long as they could reach each other they exchanged smokes, and wiped their weeping eyes.

The usual man who is "always late" was on

hand and was tossed on board and his bundle pitched after him. His hat, a good straw one, was lost overboard, but with a worthy desire to save it one of the Kanakas took a dive and swam out and captured it and bore it triumphantly back to the deck.

These natives are the greatest water dogs in the world, and as much at home in the water as a fish. Some of the stories of their power of endurance in swimming are astonishing. One, well vouched for, is about a boatload of them being capsized between the islands and swimming to the nearest shore, a distance of twenty-eight miles. The sea is always choppy and rough in the channel. Beginning to feel a little uncomfortable, and in the light of past experience, I concluded to "go below." Laid myself quickly down on my bed and remained there. My companion came in looking very brave, anticipating none of my trouble. He sought his writing paper with rather a superior air, but in about ten minutes came back again a different man and tumbled into his bunk with that don't-care expression that goes with such condition.

About eight o'clock in the morning we found

ourselves sailing along the Island of Hawaii with the great mountains of Mauna-loa and Mauna-kea in close view. We ran into the harbor of Mahukona, where for three hours we watched the natives taking off freight. One must remember that on these eight islands there is only one port where vessels can come up to the dock, and that, of course, is Honolulu. Everywhere else passengers and all kinds of freight are taken off in boats. The steamers carry very large heavy boats, and they have to battle with surf and heavy seas. A horse was taken aboard. He was led into the water and towed, swimming along with the tide, being careful to keep his nose above water, and on reaching the steamer ropes were put about him and hitched to the steam derrick, and before the horse knew where he was he was dangling in the air and plumped on deck.

After stopping at Mahukona we steamed on about ten miles into the bay of Kawaihae, where we were to land. We could only see a few small houses; (you must not suppose because a place has a name it is a town.) The steamer was anchored and we were put into one of the small boats and rowed ashore. We could not quite reach the shore, so the natives pulled the boat as near as they could and I stood up on the bow and when the waves went out jumped for the beach. Timed it wrong, however, landing in the water, the consequence being a good ducking; such things do not count here. The natives are all barefoot. The doctor was picked up by a stalwart native and carried dry to shore.

We expected to find two horses here from Mrs. Lyons, of Waimea; but they were not on hand, and as we found no natives who could speak English, were obliged to await the turn of events. There were twelve miles of up-hill riding before us before we could reach our lodgings that night. Presently a native handed me a letter from Mrs. Lyons saying to go to John Parker's place, (a half white) and wait.

So the men again took us in the boat and towed us across the harbor to the seaside cottage of John Parker, who has a large ranch on the island. He welcomed us cordially, gave us clean water, towels, etc., everything neat and clean, and we waited for our horses. His wife, a large dark native woman, was seated under a cocoanut tree surrounded with native men and women servants talking and doing nothing.

The native women of her kind seem never to lose their taste for their own people and seem to have no pride in dress or appearance. All the men and women seem to be on good terms with their mistress, and she looked no more favored than the others, except that she sat in a straw chair, while the others sat on the stone wall or on the ground.

Mr. Parker asked us if we would like a drink of cocoanut milk. One of the natives walked up to a tree in the grove and procured some ripe cocoanuts, which were opened for us and we each drank a pint of delicious cool milk: fancy this on a warm day by the seashore! The doctor took out his camera and photographed the group; there seemed to be some anxiety among the young women to secure good places, and one very good looking young woman took off her hat, I presume to show her head of black glossy hair, black as an Indian's.

About four o'clock the horses came and without saddles or bridles. After some trouble and a great deal of talking and questioning, we found saddle and bridle for one of our horses and made the boy who brought the horses give up his and ride back the twelve miles he had just come, bareback, with a rope in the horse's mouth for a bridle, making a twenty-four hours' ride for the youth. He did not seem to mind it at all, and on the way up he was about one half of the time standing up on his horse, or squatting on his haunches.

There seems to be no "tire out" to these people either in riding or swimming. We bade Mr. Parker good-bye and started up the mountains. My horse was lazy, and I was obliged to do a great deal of work with my large spur, as we were to ascend three thousand feet in twelve miles; we could not do more than walk; road was fair, though rather rocky in some places. When we reached the plateau on which Waimea stands it was about dark, and we could not have kept the road but for the guidance of the boy.

We reached Mrs. Lyons' about seven, and found them expecting us, having been acquainted by telephone of our coming. The telephone is much used on the islands, there being no telegraph, and the arrival of a visitor is telephoned on before. I was somewhat tired, and after a good smoke turned in for a night's rest.

Mrs. Lyons is a charming hostess, advanced

in years. She lives here with her two unmarried daughters, and they have never been off the Islands. One of the daughters is post-mistress, and has a little school of native children. They lived until lately in a straw house; part of it still remains. Mr. Lyons was the first missionary and translated most of the hymns now in use in most of the churches. These three ladies live all alone. Have family worship morning and night. I took my turn at reading two verses from the Bible at a time, and one of the ladies read a hymn. I shall propose the singing of it. The air is cooler here than lower down the mountain and on the shore. We have engaged horses to carry us to Laupahoehoe on the coast; about thirty-five miles from there we go to Hilo, the second largest town on the Islands, and from there we make the Volcano Kilauea.

You may suppose yourself standing where I am now writing, on the veranda, looking across the grassy plain about twelve miles, dotted with little ravines and clumps of trees. Small enclosures of stone fence mark the homes of the ranch owner natives. Horses and cattle are grazing over the plain and the whole beautiful and green. In the distance are the great mountains Mauna-loa and Mauna-kea; the snow lies deep on their summits. From Mauna-loa there was an outbreak and flow of lava some years ago, 1859. As Mrs. Lyons describes it, a red river of fire slowly moving to the sea, which it reached in about two weeks. The latest flow and the active crater are on the other side of Mauna-loa, and the flow of lava in 1881 was toward Hilo. The crater of Kilanea that visitors make is toward Hilo and only about four thousand feet up the mountain side. The regular excursion is by boat from Honolulu. We shall probably go from Hilo by horse. The "Vandalia" has gone to Hilo. Her officers are to make the volcano in squads. We shall very likely meet them there.

The language of the Islands consists in its construction, seemingly of a succession of vowels. For instance the numeral twenty-eight reads Kaiwakaluakumamawalu; a long word, but very musical, rightly pronounced. The little hymn, "Jesus loves me," in Kanaka language is "He aloha ko Jesu;" the chorus, "Keike aloha," last line, "Keike aloha. O, Jesu."

I do not acquire much of the language, however. I forgot to tell you that the day we left Honolulu the American Minister took a party of us to the palace, a large fine-looking building occupying a large square, with a high stone wall around it, gate on each side and native soldiers in white on guard. We saw only the first floor, consisting of throne room forty to seventy feet square. Two thrones on a dais with drapery over them. A red carpet in the centre and red curtains over glass frames around the room, for the different decorations belongings to the king. Rather plain furnishings, but all quite imposing. The room is large and hung with portraits of the royal family, Kamehameha I, Queen Emma, and others. On the other side of the hall is the reception room, handsomely furnished in blue. Back of it, with large folding doors, is the state dining room; the size of the room, the large silver epergnes and paintings of royal potentates make it an imposing room. There is a fine statue of Kamehameha I in front of the government building. He is represented with a helmet and feather "kohela," with malo (or girdle) and sandles on his feet: a grim smile on his face. That is all

IOLANI PALACE GROUNDS.

he has on. The helmet is the old Grecian shape and made of feathers. I saw one in the museum, which Governor Dominis (Governor of Oahu) told me was worn by a high chief. The feathers were small and laid on like scales of a fish. The original royal feather was yellow. Only two on a bird, and not to be found now. A curio shop in Honolulu has a "lay" (or band) made of them, for which they paid one hundred dollars. The Queen offered one hundred and fifty dollars for it, but they valued it higher. It is about two feet long and two inches wide.

Must have our horses and outfit photographed before we finish our ride. In my last I sent a leaf and flower; the perfume may last. There are many fragrant flowers and leaves about us everywhere.

ECHOES OF A KINGDOM.

WAIMEA, HAWAII, March 17th, 1888.

In my last letter I forgot to mention a little incident attending our stay with Mrs. Lyons. I mentioned that one of her daughters is post-mistress, and the natives come up here for their mail. The family are also called upon to doctor the natives, who are very childish about sickness, and the little post-office room in the house is well supplied with medicine. As I write a burley Kanaka is telling his wants to Miss Elizabeth, who proceeds to pour out some doctor's stuff and give him directions.

Apropos of doctoring, a very curious incident occurred the day before yesterday, and also proved very fortunate for one poor fellow. As we were lounging about and reading after dinner a request came from the coroner and police justice for the doctor to come over to the courthouse and see about a man who had been poisoned. He went over and was gone about two hours, and returned to Mrs. Lyons for some bottles and other things. It seems that a man, a Portuguese herder working for a man named Reeves, fell from his horse and died at once. He had had trouble with his employer, and was an important witness against him in a suit that was pending. Just before his death the man drank half a bottle of cold coffee, and every one at once said he was poisoned by Reeves. There was no doctor within twenty-five miles, so the coroner sent for Dr. A., who after making all possible inquiry decided to have a post mortem. Of course there were no surgical instruments at hand, so he proceeded to utilize the man's own cattle knife, an implement the herders all carry, together with the steel for sharpening. The natives are very superstitious and nearly all left, the sheriff included. The doctor cut him open and discovered that death was caused by anuerism of the heart; no doubt to the great relief of Reeves, who would otherwise have been arrested and dealt with summarily. They buried the dead man in some spot back of the old church.

The original missionaries who came out fifty years ago were very successful and converted many natives. The descendants of that generation are not keeping it up to any extent, and churches that used to be packed, as for instance the one at Hilo holding five thousand people, is now almost deserted. The descendants of the missionaries do not continue as their fathers and mothers began. They have found places under the government, also in trade, and today the leading merchants of Honolulu are of missionary origin. King Kalakauai was obliged, last July, to give the people a new constitution, though the monarchy was continued. There was a mass meeting at Honolulu (The Paris of the Islands) and a committee of thirteen formed to demand of the king the dismissal of Gibson, the Prime Minister. The city was under arms and things were serious. The king became frightened and granted all they asked. After an election affairs passed into the hands of the reform party. In this the missionary element predominated. They are virtually in power. Some trouble is expected in May, when the legislature meets again. I do not know what will be the outcome of all this. Business is not prosperous here and there is great complaint; certainly not a very bright outlook for the future.

IAO VALLEY.——WAILUKU.

Nothing can be expected from the natives. They are very lazy, good-natured people; will not work as the Chinese and Portuguese do. Disease is carrying them off rapidly. Native population has decreased from 100,000 to 40,000 within thirty or forty years. They must certainly die out. A number of white men have married natives and nothing strange is thought of it.

I shall probably visit Mr. Walbridge at his sugar plantation at Wailuku, Maui; I met him at the hotel at Honolulu. Shall probably go there while Dr. Andrews visits his old home and looks up memories of childhood.

ECHOES OF A KINGDOM.

*"An emerald isle in a setting of gold;
With its city at rest by the sea."*

HILO, HAWAII, Saturday, March 24, '83.

A very interesting place, the second in importance on the Islands. My last letters were written a week or more ago, at Waimea, on the other side of the Island, and as I look at these great mountains on the other side, I think of Mrs. Lyons and her daughters, a little sadly, although they seem content and happy. They have never been off the Island and have no thought of ever seeing the world, or even a small part of its people. Their lives have been a continual sense of duty, but they seem to be content and happy. They are well read and well posted in missionary work. They read the *Missionary Herald*, and tend and teach the few Kanakas around them.

They were very kind; they seem to enjoy the rarity of a visit from a stranger, and begged me to stay longer. Therefore, I stayed until last Monday. One of the ladies brought out a box of old stamps and gave me some of her best samples. These I shall send home. She also brought me a little piece of white silk, a part of the royal robe of the great Queen of Kamehameha I; also peaceful Kapa material used in the earlier times for her infant wrappings; it is made from wood.

Just as we were about mounting our horses for the long ride, she also gave me a little book containing a map of the Islands and a little package addressed to you, which no doubt contains a number of curios from among her treasures. We had engaged our horses and a man to drive them back and they should have been on hand at eight o'clock; the weather had cleared finely and we were anxious to be off.

Waimea is one of the cold spots and a driving mist of cloud, not quite rain, is usual there. The horses came about nine. The road was over a bleak plateau and the way was stormy and muddy. The few trees visible were devoid of foliage, they having been blighted by the grazing of the cattle. So for many a mile we rode, picking our way through the stony and muddy places. When we came to the approach of the descent on the other side the green trees and luxuriant foliage appeared again. We stopped to take a photograph of a rare tree. We were supplied with a pair of canvas saddle-bags, which were slung over the pommel, and the rubber coats and leggings were tied to the rings of the saddle in case it should rain.

We reached the sugar plantation at 12:30; stopped at John Chinaman's for dinner, and then mounted again and rode up the coast a mile to see the magnificent valley Waipeo. This is an undulation in the coast half a mile wide, running back three or four miles, the bottom level and flat, covered with rice fields. Houses dotted here and there, all looking like a toy village, as you look from the bluff about 1200 feet high into the valley. We descended by a zigzag road cut in the mountain side that looks no wider than a foot-path, very stony and very steep; perpendicular cliff on the left and a deep valley on the right. I went down only two-thirds of the way on my horse. He seemed to be afraid to go over the steep places, and I was quite tired with spurring and urging. He was not a good beast for this kind of work.

Doctor kept on to the bottom of the cliff and took some photographs. While they were taking the photos I lighted my pipe and threw myself on the grass and let my horse graze, he having had nothing to eat all day. While I was resting here the schoolmaster joined me and we had a chat. Becoming tired, I mounted and rode back to the town and waited some time before they returned. Meanwhile I learned that Mr. Horner, the planter, was expecting us, Judge Lyman having telephoned that we were coming. As the next stop was sixteen miles further on, I persuaded the Doctor that it was time to start.

We rode out to this pretty cottage, where we were kindly received. He owns about one thousand acres of sugar cane. Had a charming stay with Mr. and Mrs. Horner; such hospitality I shall never forget. We mounted again, and after a hard ride of sixteen miles up one side of the gulch and down the other, a steep and stony route brought us to Honaka, Mr. Lyman's ranch. We passed a steep gulch, as they call them here. They are really indentations in the cliff, opening gradually to the ocean and running back quite a little distance, and the descent is anywhere from 200 to 500 feet.

We met Mr. Lyman on the road and reached his home a little after noon. He is a very fine looking white man with white hair and moustache. His native wife came out on the porch to greet us. Her voice is soft and she is polite and polished. She wore the inevitable "holoku." They have thirteen children, ten of whom are living. Three or four little people were at the table, they have the Caucasian of the father. They have prayers, attended by children and all. About seven o'clock every evening Mr. L. conducts this service, playing the melodian. Mr. L. brought out some native songs and we sang. We rode to a couple of sugar mills, which occupied a part of the afternoon, and then had a good night's rest in a pleasant room on the first floor. We took some photographs of the house and family. Mr. L. has recently been appointed a judge. We were off at 8:30 for Laupahoehoe, up and down gulches. At the bottom of one big one we found a group of Kanakas resting their horses. As the doctor took their photographs, they became interested. One man explained to another that one of us was a doctor. One of the older ones sent a boy to the house for his mother, who was suffering with a tumor. She came and squatted down in a most phlegmatic manner. Doctor examined it, and through one of the men told her husband that nothing could be done for her, medicine no good, and if the knife was used it would kill her. They took the information stolidly. She reached out to her husband for his pipe and began smoking, not a word of comment at her death warrant.

We reached Laupahoehoe, where we expected to take a boat for Hilo, and found it was a day late; so as our contract for horses was out, our man started back at once and we settled down to spend a day at the port of Laupahoehoe, where we expected to take the steamer "Kinau" and go on to Hilo, a distance of about thirty miles. We therefore started out to find lodgings for our unexpected stay, there being no taverns of any kind for the accommodation of strangers. We made the acquaintance of the manager of the sugar mills, and with his help found a native woman with a Scotch husband who would give us a room, so we scattered for a time to look over the place. It is at the foot of cliffs 500 or 600 feet high, having the only safe little harbor where they can load sugar, and has become the landing place for boats. They were loading a small steamer with sugar, so I laid myself down on a grassy knoll and watched the Kanakas work. They do it with a rush. The sugar is all put up at the mills in bags of one hundred pounds. These are piled on the dock from the warehouse and the boats come from the steamer; heavy large boats each manned with five natives, bags pitched in and rowed out. As I have said before, the natives are regular water dogs and pull these immense boats with five tons of sugar in and out through the surf. It was very quiet that day, but sometimes the boats are swamped; this the natives care nothing for, as they cannot be drowned, but it wets the sugar.

The sugar as shipped from the mill is of a light brown color. Very nice, and except that the U. S. tariff prevents its entry above a certain degree of whiteness, could be washed through the centrifugals to a color as white as our coffee sugar and sent into the market without going to a refinery. One of the sugar boilers showed us some. The sugar after granulating is poured into centrifugals, which are about as large as washtubs, double, the inner one revolving with great rapidity, and made of perforated copper. The molasses is thrown through it and comes down between the cylinders, leaving a clear white sugar, dry and ready for bagging, at the bottom. The operator took a small rubber tube, and while the cylinder was revolving, merely threw a tiny spray of water into it. This washed the color off the brown sugar, and I reached in and took a handful of clear, white, handsome sugar from it. But this they are not allowed to export.

After watching the loading for a time, I walked on the lava crags to secure a place where they do not fear sharks, and watched the native boys riding the surf. Each has a board a little wider than an ironing board and about the same length. They wade out, going through the rollers until they see a big one coming in, and catch it, jumping on their boards as a boy jumps on his sled and they ride on the top of the wave. The feet of the natives seem to be tough, and women and boys wear no shoes and walk on the stony, sharp rocks without any apparent fear of stone bruises. A group of natives stood in a circle on the shore and watched the sport.

I saw one right pretty native woman, dressed

in a red "holoku" and the usual flat-brimmed straw hat, trimmed with red garlands, start for the shore. She was very much dressed up, having shoes and stockings on. As she could not afford to risk the shoes and stockings, she deliberately sat down, proceeded to divest herself of her cherished pedal covering, and then walked in on the crags, carefully carrying the same in her hands, preparatory to her swim in the surf. Supper at the Chinaman's.

In the morning Dr. A. found a man with a good horse which he would sell for $65, and as we had to provide ourselves with them at Hilo for the volcano trip, could either rent the animal and send him back again, or buy him and sell him again. He concluded to take the horse and ride on to Hilo along the coast while I would wait and take the "Kinau" the next day. So we started with our bundles for our lodgings. You can imagine a woodshed boarded up on the open side, whitewashed inside, two beds about three feet apart; neat bedclothes, lace of some kind on the pillow (a decoration never omitted no matter what kind the bed,) and the bed itself—its hardness I cannot describe. A piece of matting laid on the floor would have been a

NATIVE STRAW HOUSE.——MODERN HOUSE.

downy couch in comparison. This gorgeous apartment was reached by walking through a narrow hall between two Chinese houses and then along a board platform. We retired to our beds and for two hours wrestled with our bones. The bed was so hard and generally insufferable, words are inadequate to express it; so neither said a word. Could not sleep of course and found myself laughing and shaking to hear my companion toss and mutter.

Finally I ventured the remark that we were simply a couple of quiet American travelers abroad for pleasure and the benefit of our health. "How are you getting along?"

The reply was, "This is awful!"

We sat up and found that by folding up the gorgeous red and white cover matters might be improved, then proceeded to find out "where that draught came from," and found that the roof was open about four feet above the wall, therefore into this opening we stuffed our rubber coats and leggings, and finally our tired bones could stand it no longer and we slept. Had breakfast at the Chinaman's. Doctor started for Hilo on horseback and I settled down to spend the day. Passed a pleasant hour with the postmaster, and from his wife procured an easy chair when I wished to sit on the steps and smoke. The great lava crags, dashed by the surf, stretched out far into the sea about twenty-five or thirty feet. Across the street was a spring, and here all the morning, Portuguese women were going to and fro, as this seemed to be their wash-day; setting the baby (if they had one) up against a rock, and placing the bottle of milk with tube in proper shape for its sustenance, proceeded to rub the clothes on the stones which answered for wash tubs. Portuguese women carry all loads on their heads. Are erect and have fine figures.

I climbed a road up a cliff about six hundred feet and was rewarded with a fine view from this elevation. Then came down and amused myself looking at the assistant postmaster try to shoot a rooster which was to serve for his dinner. He chased it all over the place with his gun. Finally, with the help of his wife, chased it into a corner and finished him. He was very proud of his success and boasted to me that he hit him four times, and spoke farther of his game. I remarked that their way was different from ours. We generally caught the chicken out in the yard and wrung its neck, a much more simple way, but one very much less exciting. He had been two hours at it and said he was pretty tired and thought he would take a bath. So he meandered out to a cavity of rock fifteen feet square and five deep, safe from sharks. I could have gone also, but remembering that my feet were not tough enough to stand lava rocks, I refrained. He did not ask me to dinner, so I called on my friend John and dined on the same viands as before. This menu seems to be the only one Johnnie has. After dinner as I had about exhausted the frivolities of the place, I secured a nice piece of wood and sat down on the steps to whittle and the postmaster sat down beside me, and I answered all his questions about the United States. Gradually the stick I was whittling assumed the shape of a boat and I became interested. I noticed I was the centre of absorbing interest of about a dozen Kanaka boys, whose greedy eyes were fixed on the boat and "hope springing eternal in their breasts" that I would name the happy possessor. To increase the interest I walked off toward the mill, the boys followed, running, quarreling and generally indicating that they were with me to stay until the fate of that boat was decided. To quell the excitement, I put the boat in my pocket and the crowd gradually thinned out, leaving one urchin glaring at me from the top of a candle box in the grocery store. I kept the boat as a memento. If it stays with me until I reach home S. B. shall have it.

The longest day has an end and about eight in the evening the "Kinau" came in. I bade Laupahoehoe a fond farewell, tumbled into a boat and went on board the steamer. The purser kindly gave me a good room on the upper deck, and after getting my traps aboard and putting my letters into the bag for Honolulu to go by the next mail, I turned in for a good night's rest. We reached Hilo about eleven o'clock that night. As the steamer did not leave until ten the next morning I spent the night there, and rising at six the next morning found myself looking out on the beautiful bay of Hilo, a semicircle of beach fringed with cocoanut trees and the pretty little town on "that emerald isle, with its city at rest by the sea," and the two giants, Mauna-kea and Mauna-loa looming up in the clouds in the dis-

HULA DANCE.

tance, their snow-covered peaks against the blue background of sky, and the whole enveloped in the soft, warm velvet atmosphere, truly a sight for the immortals. To breathe this air was simply an elixir. Making my toilet very deliberately, my stateroom door wide open, I could see the excursionists going ashore in the early boats; but I have learned something of travel and waited for a good breakfast and a chat with the captain, taking it leisurely, and finally bundled myself and traps into the last boat. I was pulled up on deck by some Kanakas, and was accosted by a pleasant gentleman who informed me that Dr. Andrews had arrived the evening before, and was looking for me, and that we were expected to visit Judge Austin, and his carriage was waiting to take me up, and so I was driven to the house.

I gave Dr. A. his letters and returned to the post-office for mine. A conversation with the postmaster developed the fact that my mail had been delivered to a very prominent resident of Hilo, bearing my name in full, minus the M. D. He is one of the old residents here. I found my way to his office, a frame house near the bay, and it was closed. The Portuguese barber across the way told me that the doctor had not been down that morning, so I sat down on a box across the narrow street and gazed curiously at my name on the weather beaten sign over the way. Of course I was impatient, and fifteen minutes more found me climbing the hill to his house, a pretty cottage in real Hawaiian style, with open windows giving glimpses of artistic interior. The Doctor was out and a lady volunteered to find him. Shortly afterward he emerged from one of the little cottages in the vicinity. We gazed at each other rather curiously, he giving his name, and I introducing myself as bearing his name from a far off land. There were numerous explanations, etc., with his hearty "I am glad to see you, sir; I have seven letters and some papers for you." Continuing, he said that he had opened one and found it began "Dear Papa," and as he was not aware of any children in the States, was about to take the letters back to the office. He is a handsome, intelligent elderly gentleman, with gray hair and polished manners and very cordial ways. He said he was about taking his bath and I could read my letters and we would walk down the street together.

When I had finished reading home letters I felt ten years younger, and went out into the open air like a refreshed giant.

Yesterday I drifted about the place; Judge Austin walked with me and introduced me to nearly all the prominent men there—lawyers, judges, etc. Today is Sunday. Went to church, a pretty little structure partly filled with whites and natives. The choir sang Faure's "Palm Trees," as it was Palm Sunday; the choir intoned the Lord's Prayer. The church was beautifully trimmed with palms of many kinds. A good sermon by the pastor on that day. Quite a number of English people are stopping at Judge Austin's. There was quite a jolly gathering at dinner.

Was waited on by a committee yesterday and asked to make an address at a temperance meeting; declined with thanks, telling them that the Doctor had promised to do all the public speaking, while I attended to the necessary writing. We attended the native church service tonight, where was a very interesting gathering of Sunday School children, who sang in a way that would put to shame any attempts of the kind in our own goodly city. The boys sang alone two pieces, one of them the "Holy, Holy, Lord God Almighty." There were about fifty boys in the chorus, who with their melodious voices made music well worth listening to. Have been well trained and I am told can sing the Hallelujah chorus very well. I am going to hear it tomorrow. Monday morning about nine o'clock I went to the native school to attend the opening exercises. About forty boys, in age from nine to twenty years, are in school. First was a selection played by the brass band under the trees, consisting of about a dozen boys old and young, and they played well. Then back into the house where the boys sang "Holy, holy," and read the Bible, etc. Mr. Burt led the meeting. What do you suppose? Why, the Hallelujah Chorus from the Messiah was sung, and I never heard it sung better. Fancy a lot of natives and half castes singing this without words or music before them and without a break or error. I was astonished.

Dr. A. and Dr. Wetmore came up with the horses and we started for a visit up the ravine on horseback, taking in Rainbow Falls and the other sights. I cannot describe this ride in detail, but I never expect to take such another rough ride again. The rugged slopes and gulches, the steep sides covered thick with underbrush, long grass; jumping over fallen trees; fairly sliding down steep, muddy streams not over a foot wide; overhanging trees knocking our hats off and projecting limbs trying to break our legs. All this at an angle of forty-five degrees, and coming to a perpendicular wall four feet high, the horses standing straight up and jumping so that all you can do is to cling to the the saddle and try not to fall off backwards. Crossing from boulder to boulder, and then having to come back through it all in a drizzling rain.

I have been told since by old travelers here that they seldom try to ride it, but leave the animals at the worst places and walk. I think it must have been arranged especially for us "haoulis," but we accepted the situation and never flinched.

Reached home about six o'clock, and in the evening went to the meeting of the Scientific Club. The next evening accepted an invitation to Judge Lyman's for dinner, and met the most influential element here. Yesterday, at Mrs. Lyman's suggestion, both her family and Judge

Austin's went over to Cocoanut Island, a most lovely place, reached partly by boat and partly by horse. We dismounted, rowing through the surf and then bestriding horses, riding around the bay where we were taken across in a boat to the island, an ideal one for a picnic, covered with tall cocoanut trees, the lava crags stretching out in broken patches toward the sea between beautiful ponds of water and white sandy beach, fine for bathing. A comfortable house used for camping purposes on the island. After a plunge in the surf, the Kanaka boy built a fire of dried banana and cocoanut leaves and boiled the coffee, and with fine appetites we managed to dispose of a most excellent repast. Took some photos and reached town again about six o'clock.

We planned our ride to the volcano, and Dr. Wetmore intended to go with us, but may not be able to on account of the illness of his grandchild. Am sorry, as I suppose there is no one better posted than he. From the crater we take a different route to Punaluu, where we expect to take the boat and go to the Island of Maui to visit Mr. Walbridge at the Wailuku plantation, and then Dr. Andrews will keep on with his horse to his home at Kailua for a visit of a week or so.

Next Sunday will be Easter Sunday, and I will probably be at the volcano, in the midst of its marvels. With the "blue ethereal" above me and the fiery gulf below, and the walk in the valley among the crags of black lava that they tell of, I shall imagine myself as standing betwixt Heaven and the Valley of the Inferno.

ECHOES OF A KINGDOM.

EXTRACT FROM HISTORY OF KAAHUMANU, FAVORITE WIFE OF KAMEHAMEHA.

"She was born about the year 1773 at the foot of the hill Kauiki, on the Eastern shore of Maui. Her father was Keeaumaku, a distinguished warrior. Her mother was Namahaua, the daughter of King Kekaulike and had been Queen of Maui. Soon after her birth her parents removed to Hawaii, where she narrowly escaped drowning in infancy. She was riding with her parents on the pola, or top of a double canoe, wrapped in a roll of white copper, or cloth, as they were sailing along the coast. From the tossing of the canoe she fell off into the sea fast asleep. The white copper floating on the waves attracted the attention of her parents. They paddled quickly back and drew her out of the water.

"Once when following her mother around the end of a canoe on the seashore a huge wave

KAAHUMANU.

carried her out. A cousin sprang in and rescued her. The years of her infancy were years of wars and bloodshed between the kings of the different islands. Trained in heathenism and on the battlefield, Kaahumanu at the age of thirteen was taken among the wives of Kamehameha I, and being of high birth, was held in great esteem in the eyes of the nation and her husband. She became the favorite of the conqueror, although he had twenty other wives. Though the favorite, she had often to endure his anger and experienced insults at his iron hand. They were reconciled at the solicitation of Vancouver. During one difficulty she determined to leave him and embarked alone in a beautiful canoe for Kauai. She was pursued and brought back. Kamehameha was a man of violence. Nothing would appease his wrath and he once beat Kaakumanu with an iron anvil for speaking of a young man as 'handsome.' He was jealous and fond of her, and once put forth an edict that if any one should insult her, he should be put to death.

"At Kamehameha's death she was made a Premier and virtually ruled the kingdom. She became a Christian in 1824, was married to the

King of Hawaii, and died in June, 1832, a devout Christian, repeating these lines of a native hymn:

"'Lo, here am I, O Jesus, grant me thy gracious smile.'"

ECHOES OF A KINGDOM.

VOLCANO HOUSE, HAWAII, Apr. 6, '88.

We left Hilo Sunday morning on horseback, Dr. Chas. H. Wetmore with us, and started for an up-hill rocky ride of thirty miles. It had been raining and bad weather for some days, but the start of our ride was propitious, and for the first ten miles the weather and the sky were all that could be desired, and the two doctors gathered flowers and ferns to their hearts' content; they being very well versed in botany, were of course delighted with every new specimen of fern or flower along the route. But rain came, and for the rest of the day we soaked and sweltered in our rubber coats and leggings, and such a ride and such a road! If such a thing were possible, this road was rougher than anything we had yet experienced. We could not stop for lunch as there was no place to do so, and we munched our hard tack and boiled eggs as we rode in the driving mist.

We reached the Volcano House at 5:30, having made a straight ride of thirty miles, except to pick some kukua nuts or some new find among the shrubs, etc. Our horses would take a bit of grass once in a while and eat as they went, and so we made it, and as there was a stretch of good road and level for a mile near the house, we came up to the hotel on a gallop and in good shape, but oh, how stiff we were! nine and one-half hours in the saddle. My clothes were stripped off and put in the drying room. Thanks to our oilcloth, our underwear was comparatively dry.

After a hearty supper, and a good smoke before the large brick fire-place, wound up the day by retiring for the night in a front room with windows looking out on the great crater of Kilauea, too tired with the trip to realize our wonderful surroundings. The next day was still foggy and rainy, but we visited the sulphur bank and took a sulphur steam bath in natural steam coming up from a crack in the rock. The next day (yesterday) looked dubious until about noon, when the weather appeared more favorable, and after dinner we started for the crater with guide, lanterns, walking sticks, canteens of water, etc. The road leads down the cliff in front of the house, 260 feet high, where we reached the floor of the crater, and then began a two-mile tramp across the bed of lava to the active crater. I cannot give you any idea of this curious and great field of old lava, but you can imagine an ocean with a good sized storm on, and all the waves a congealed and hardened mass of great black hills and valleys, seamed with great cracks and slabs of the black rock appearing in all directions. This is surrounded by high cliffs from 450 to 1,000 feet high, like an amphitheater. On one side of it is the active part of the crater, and one must see it all, as words fail to describe the scene. The centre of all is the cone of the Halemaumau where fires are burning, and around this great crater cone smaller ones are burning. Some have filled up with lava thrown out and fallen in, showing great caverns fifty or sixty feet deep. Took photos in two or three places, then skirted around the lava to the burning lake. We found a point on the edge of the cliff about 3,000 feet from the lake and about fifty feet above it, and the sight cannot easily be forgotten.

The lake is yet active and a good deal of it has fallen in and sunk and the surface cannot be traversed. This one as we saw it was nearly semi-circular, 350 feet in diameter and filled nearly to the brim with lava. It was playing like a fountain at different points. The surface of dark purple lava was thrown thirty feet in the air and fountains of the red hot lava played for a few moments, subsided, then gathered strength and again boiled and threw off this magnificent fountain. This was going on at five different places at once. Then a circle of red could be seen around the edge, gradually creeping across the lake, soon to burst up in red spray high in the air. It was not crimson or scarlet, nor like the red light of a blast furnace, but a fiery intense red.

We sheltered ourselves behind some upturned lava slabs over a steam hole where we could keep warm, and here we stayed and watched the gorgeous coloring of purple and red in the hissing billows of hot lava dashing against the dark cliffs or rocks of lava; here and there a yellow whirlpool or a golden colored river would steal over the surface of the lake.

From where we rested, once a boiling cauldron of molten lava, the magnificence of the sight cannot be depicted on canvas, nor can the half be told. The red light tinted the vast clouds of escaping smoke and steam that were constantly issuing from the cones or fissures about; night was drawing near and darkness settled down on the great dark plain.

The hotel was two miles away, and then our guide became of great importance to us, as we had not the slightest idea of the trail in this dark place. Lanterns were lighted, staffs taken up, overcoats buttoned up, and we turned our backs on the glorious sight. Our guide kept his path unerringly across the black plain. Great care must be taken not to catch one's foot in a crack, as the lava is sharp and glassy and every step must be watched. We were an hour and a half reaching the foot of the cliff. Only one accident, one of our party stepped into a crack and cut his foot on the sharp edge of the lava rock. At the foot of the cliff we found our horses, which we had sent down, as the climb up the 500 feet after the hard tramp to the crater must have been very hard for them. I mounted and with my lantern started on ahead. My horse was a little dazed and restive at the unusual situation, and I found that I was not familiar with the turns in the narrow and zigzaggy road, so I was a little sorry I did not wait. When about a third way up Dr. Wetmore, who was riding a little behind me, called out that Dr. Andrews should have a lantern, and a moment after there seemed to be some trouble back of us. The guide and the Portuguese were both back there, and as I stopped and looked, I could see the form of a white horse with no saddle on, and presently the horse came tearing up to where I was. Mr. Maby, who was back of me, caught him or he might have pushed my horse over the verge. However, no harm proved to have been done. The girth of his saddle broke and the rider rolled off his horse, fortunately on the inside, and the horse, tripped by the saddle, fell and then started up the road. The rider was not injured, and after repairing the damage, we continued on our way.

Out of the darkness, the sight indelibly imprinted on our vision, we emerged to welcome the cheery light and warmth of the hotel, reaching there about nine P. M.; we wrote our names in the big book, wherein poets and travelers, nobility and every day people like ourselves had written their names in turn, many having jotted impressions of the great Kilauea. Farewell mighty Kilauea, with your molten sea and your picture rocks; would that I might again view thy wonders. This will never be my lot, however, so it is farewell to Kilauea forever. Perhaps you have forgotten the dimensions of this crater; it is oval in shape, nine miles in circumference and six thousand feet above sea level.

Tomorrow we shall ride in another direction to the ocean and Punaluu. We will dismiss our horses and take boat for Maaleia Bay and go to Wailuku, where I shall visit Mr. Walbridge. Dr. Andrews goes to Kailua. A very pleasant visit at Hilo; it is a charming city, and was delightfully entertained at Judge Austin's. While there received a note from the clergyman, asking me to sing at the Union meeting Sunday evening. I inspected the stock of music in use there, which was very limited. I found "Gems of Songs" and arranged the words of "Jesus Lover of my Soul" to the air of "When the Swallows Homeward Fly," and sang it to the accompaniment of a poula organ. By the way, I heard at a blue ribbon meeting, while at Hilo, a half-white girl play the zither very well. I must close as it is growing dark. The wife of the manager of this house is a half white and the children varied in complexion. I enclose a fern found on the cliff. Look at it through the magnifying glass.

The great god, Maui, laid there his nets and snared the sun, as he rose, only releasing him upon his promise to always bestow light and warmth upon the Islands.

KING KALAKAUA.

ECHOES OF A KINGDOM.

WAILUKU, MAUI, April 13th, 1888.

Still on the Islands, but headed homeward, however. That is, we are going, next week, to Honolulu, sailing some time during May, on Steamer "Australia." I cannot give you a detailed account of all I have seen, but the three islands of Oahu, Maui and Hawaii we have made quite thoroughly on horseback. I am spending a few days with Mr. Walbridge, manager of this plantation, he has about one thousand acres under his care, is on horseback at five o'clock in the morning, overseeing.

On one of these early morning rides I noticed a native dragging himself wearily along and my companion informed me that he was a victim of the "Hoodoo," that nothing could rouse him from his apathy. His enemy had willed him to die, and die he must.

The mountain containing the extinct crater of Hale-a-ka-la "House of the Sun" forms East

Maui, the largest extinct volcano of the world. Maui is also noted as containing extensive sugar plantations, the famous Spreckles owns an extensive one here. The view from the highest point of Maui is very fine, Oahu in the dim distance, Molokai across the water and the extinct crater that I mentioned is twenty-five or thirty miles in circumference, and two to three thousand feet deep and ten thousand feet above the sea level, and contains within this circumference about sixteen basins of old volcanoes. Kaui is named the Garden of the Islands, but as we are limited in time, cannot make this trip. We are due at home in the States before June.

I came by steamer from a place called Punaluu, and on the way His Majesty King Kalakaua, with his retinue from his resort at Kailua came on board, with six or eight servants. He was conveyed to steamer by his boat crew, in six-oared barge. The crew, dressed in white and blue uniform, came aboard, bade him adieu, knelt and kissed his hand. The king had two women attendants near him. One squatted down near him and lighted his cigarette for him. The other, I was told, was his body servant, and attended to his going to bed and getting up.

He had his singers and taropabeli fiddle and they tuned their instruments and sang songs the entire evening. I was much interested and took it all in.

The king sat in an arm chair and when any of the natives or servants went near him, to speak to him, they squatted down so as not to stand higher than he. In passing they would doff hats and sidle by.

At Kawaihae, where he stopped, the head man came for him in a large boat, with torches flaring, and took the party ashore. Being a free-born American citizen, and thinking the king might be glad to become acquainted with me, and also fearing that I might never again have such a chance, I took the bull by the horns, so to speak, and stepped up by the side of his chair; lifting my hat, I remarked:

"I wish to thank your Majesty for the very pleasant evening I have spent listening to the excellent singing of your band." He was very agreeable, and we had a chat about music, rowing, electric lights, cable, etc. On going ashore he shook hands very cordially, bade me good-bye, said he hoped to be back in Houolulu before I sailed, and invited me to come and see him.

Having always found it well to be friendly with kings, therefore, I shall accept his invitation.

Mr. Walbridge has put a fine horse at my disposal and I can take an airing at any time. Will write once or twice more before I start home. *Aloha.*

* * * * *

In addition to letters, I find various memoranda of the king's hospitality. His hospitality to the base-ball players is spoken of particularly, they being invited to a *luau*, or native feast, given in a tent one hundred feet long, fifty feet wide, the floor covered with rushes; the king and his guests seated on strips of matting on each side of the table, which consisted of a board a few inches from the floor. Kanaka girls were stationed about ten feet apart, dressed in white Mother Hubbards or kolokus. "These dusky symphonies in white waved lazily long-handled, gayly-colored fans over the table." Calabashes filled with native food were before each plate. On platters were baked beef, baked pork, baked chicken, baked veal, each being wrapped in the leaves in which they had been baked on stones in the earth.

To transfer the poi from the calabash to the

plate seemed the easier way toward final disposal. A pretty girl, however, laughing at the novices, dipped her pretty fingers into the pink mush and skilfully conveyed sundry twists of poi from the calabash to her mouth. Recovering from our astonishment and realizing that this was real native style and not a breach of etiquette, we followed suit and ate poi with our fingers. With music, laughter and song as accompaniments, the American base-ball team had partaken of the native Hawaiian feast and felt themselves most highly honored.

Another time we find the hospitable Kalakaua giving a dinner for the officers of the vessels in port. One was given in honor of the gallant Captain Schoonmaker, of the U. S. flag ship "Vandalia," who gave up his life in that tragedy of the Samoan sea.

In addition to these letters, I write down bits of information that have come to me, perhaps have been told many times before by others, but the subject is, however, wonderfully interesting, namely, the "Lepers of Molokai." Nature's walls hem them in on this sea-girt island; natural formations of rock make a "city's walls," and of the original chiefs who dwelt here there are only about forty descendants left to dispute with the leper community the question of "Thus far shalt thou go," etc. A few wind-breaks or stone piles are all there is left to show former ownership. The most noble work of the Hawaiian government is in its faithful care of its wards, the stricken lepers of the Islands.

Our correspondent, in his journeying over the three islands named Oahu, Maui and Hawaii, mentions seeing a group of five or six on their way to the home of the "living dead." Thus says the Hawaiian Government, "I must be cruel to be kind." The visiting board started on its customary tour of investigation at one time, in Molokai. Taking the steamer, they landed at the leper settlement, Kalapapa. The spokesman of the settlement presented their grievances, relating mostly to change of food, etc. He spoke of kind treatment, and in answer the speaker of the visiting committee assured him that these matters would be satisfactorily arranged for them. They received quite an ovation, the leper brass band of twelve pieces played for them, and their responsive "alohas" were very touching as greetings and farewells.

The committee paid a visit to the Bishop

home for girls, in charge of Sister Marianne and assistants. Their heroism was deeply appreciated and a source of wonder, as among the sterner sex of which the visiting party was composed, the desire to not linger longer than was necessary was discernible, for the sight was indeed grievous and pitiful.

At Kalawao, Fathers Conrady and Wendolin were met, they being in charge of the boy's school. The party visited the new church on the site of Father Damien's old one, also the tomb of the apostle of Molokai.

The traveler, in some one of his early letters, speaks of not caring to accept the hospitalities unadvised of a real native hut on the horseback journey through the islands mentioned, fearing very likely the possible proximity, in so doing, of some unfortunate member of a native family, stricken perhaps with the first symptom of the dread disease, whom love and protection would conceal from the authorities, hoping to gain a few days, or months' reprieve from the dreadful verdict, the necessary "edict of a kingdom."

On Father Damien's monument, presented by the National Leprosy Fund Association of England, Prince of Wales, President, are inscribed the following lines: "Greater love hath no man than this, that a man lay down his life for his friend:"

Among the interesting memoranda connected with the Hawaiian trip, the writer finds the following invitation to Iolani Palace, addressed to the traveler.

THE CHAMBERLAIN OF THE HOUSEHOLD
IS COMMANDED BY
HIS MAJESTY
TO INVITE YOU TO A
DANCE AT IOLANI PALACE
THE 2ND INST., AT 9 O'CLOCK P. M.

The reception and ball at the palace, given in honor of Sir William Wiseman, of H. R. M. S. "Caroline," was a brilliant affair. Gay uniforms of different nations, worn by brave men, also beautiful gowns worn by fair ladies, society leaders of Honolulu, the Paris of the Islands, the music of the Hawaiian band, electric lights, palms, ferns, and gorgeous flowers, formed a

PRINCESS LILIOUKALANI.

bewildering combination, a wonderful panorama to the onlooker. The gayly decked forms whirled in the mazy dance or gathered in groups. The queen wore, on this occasion, a magnificent gown of black velvet trimmed with mamo *leis*. This costume was worn by Her Majesty on the occasion of Queen Victoria's Jubilee celebration.

When I dwell upon this wonderful kaleidoscope, as it was told to me, I seem to see a procession, an apotheosis of heroes, prior to that cruel sacrifice in the waters of the relentless Samoan Sea, where noble ships and gallant men were tossed about, mere playthings of the savage winds and waves: brave sailor laddies dying like heroes, a veritable tragedy of the sea.

What a change has come over the spirit of our dream! King Kalakaua has followed his warrior ancestors to their long home, and the easy, not "uneasy" head that wore a crown, the hospitable, pleasure-loving king, rests from his earthly pleasures and perhaps the occasional frown caused by some petty revolution of short duration. Queen Kapiolani lives quietly at her home in Waikiki, a few miles from Honolulu.

Princess Kaiulani, having finished her education this year in England, has returned to Honolulu. Thus far she has escaped the trouble and care involved in the wearing of a "golden sorrow"; rumor says she may soon wed the man of her choice. If not Queen of the Isles, she will be Queen of Hearts; this little maiden of "high degree" of the year 1888. Therefore, in that picture and festive scene at Iolani palace, with its beautiful coloring, was the Sun of Royalty already drawing near the horizon, ere long to vanish from sight.

The postman's ring or knock at one's door is a "home sound" most welcome, especially when it tells of a home coming; little children's faces brighten, the steps of their elders quicken and it is then perhaps we dispense with those pathetic strains of Gungle's "Sounds from Home," and let the "Fiddle" have its swing.

It is a home coming, not a parting.

We hear the Hawaiian band for the last time as it plays the stirring "Hawaii Ponoi," or perhaps the strains of some Aloha song reach us from the Kanaka chorus; *leis* (lays) of flowers and sweet scented *maile* speed the parting guest; we are homeward bound.

Thus the traveler reached his native shore, laden with beautiful memories of a sunny land and cherished memories of newly made friends, and from Aloha Land came gifts to the "stay-at-homes." Curious shells and bits of coral, kukui jewelry, braided fans, bearing the interwoven greeting from across the Sea of "Aloha œ nui;" there were flower *leis* sent as farewells to the parting guest, shell and feather bands; old Kilauea furnished samples of lava, and with the ferns and fragrant leaves came that breath of salt air and tint of summer sky that might well tempt the invalid, or otherwise, to cross the Peaceful Sea, really a well-deserved name notwithstanding that little ebullition of temper encountered by the traveler, caused by "kona" we are assured.

In an earlier letter, the poet tells us most poetically that Madame Pacific dislikes outside interference. Now that she has settled the Kona for a few years, we may presume that she has resumed her wonted ways and wears the calm of a queen on her majestic face. Apropos of the Pacific in the present tense, what do they say of Hawaii as to tense and mood? Hawaii of late seems to be taking rapid strides toward freeing herself from even an echo of a kingdom. In the words of the old song "We may be happy yet," we dwellers of two countries, as sisters and brethren, under one flag, the glorious "Stars and Stripes."

Whatever way it may be decided, may "peace and happiness," "truth and justice," spread their wings over your beautiful Islands, ye kindly, hospitable dwellers of Hawaii. It would be indeed a new era in our history could we be permitted to celebrate a Fourth of July, or February twenty-second, among your tropical groves, and address you as "fellow citizens and countrymen." A person of the feminine persuasion naturally feels a little tendency towards a fit of ague, a little chattering of the teeth, in taking a mental survey of those ships of every nation standing about the Islands, waiting apparently for a slice.

With the "Passing of a Kingdom" goes much of the romance and legendary atmosphere and traditional customs surrounding the throne of these dusky kings and queens. The Passing of a Kingdom, however, cannot chill that balmy air, or stiffen those waving palms, nor yet dim that glorious sunshine. When the edicts of a kingdom cease to exist, the "Echoes of a Kingdom" come fainter and more faint on the listening ear, until only a memory remains.

Little Kingdom of the Sea, farewell.

ECHOES OF A KINGDOM.

A GREETING TO THE PROVISIONAL GOVERNMENT.

The writer of the little bundle of letters wherein the ink was fading, has passed on to that "other country" from whence there comes no answering "Aloha œ, aloha nui." We have said good-night to a Kingdom. In yon same fair clime may we send a greeting to the most Honorable Provisional Government of Hawaii, as you bridge the gulf 'twixt the past and the future, with your President, your Ministers, and your Legislature convening in yon Iolani palace.

Doubtless the rod of justice will rule as well, minus the feathery emblem of royalty. Prosperity seems to follow in your wake. Being related to Brother Jonathan, we naturally take an interest in matters generally. If nutmegs will not grind one way, they will another. We take an interest in the "Mills of the Gods" also, hoping they will grind exceeding well. Certainly, we must rejoice with those to whom this Provisional Government is so welcome; many are descendants of those who toiled in the service of the "Master," living and dying among those who today are reaping the benefit of their sacrifices. Some day there may come to you, Fair Hawaii, a matrimonial proposal from Uncle Sam.

In· considering this alliance, however, our much respected, honorable and elderly Uncle seems to meet with many obstacles. His numerous advisers cast a shadow over his horoscope. They indicate that to "take you by the lily white hand and lead you over the water," means too new and great a responsibility for our bachelor Uncle.

It is not impossible also that after the manner and privilege of the fair sex you may change your mind, and thus we will have a rejected suitor on our hands with an extended experience to add to his journal of events.

Therefore, wedded or single, Kingdom or Republic, live forever, Beautiful Hawaii.

PLANTS AND SHRUBS.

PLANTS AND SHRUBS IN THE GARDEN OF A HONOLULU RESIDENT.

Royal Palm,
Areca Palm Cocoanut,
Mango,
Papai,
2 Crinums,
Colocasia,
Bermuda Grass,
2 Sorrels,
Orange,
Loquat,
Ohia, a fruit tree,
Clitoria,
2 Parechites,
Plumieria,
Cape Jasmine,
3 Hibiscus,
Lime,
2 Marantas,
Climbing Arum,
Phylanthus,
Heliotrope,
Petunia,
Bamboo,
Algaroba,
Lantana,
Gaillardia,
Marigold,
Carnation,
Rondeletia,
2 Begonias,
Cryptameria,
2 Peperomias,
Ilangilang,
Wandering Jew,

Fan Palm,
Screw Pine,
Tamarind,
2 Thunbergias,
2 Amaryllis,
2 Dracoenas,
Hilo Grass,
2 Bananas,
Fig,
Alligator Pear,
Sunflower,
C. Clerodendron,
Agave,
Crape Jasmine,
Climbing Jasmine,
Pomegranate,
20 kinds of ferns,
Vanilla,
Stephanotis,
Nasturtium,
Verbena, Vorne
Periwinkle,
6 Varieties Croton,
Indigo,
Capsicum,
Calliopsis,
8 Caladiums,
A yellow flowered tree,
Sellaginella,
Saxifrage,
2 Ornamental Grasses,
Rose Apple,
Atamasco Lily,
Euclaris,

2 Colored foliage shrubs.

FRUITS.

FRUITS AND THEIR SEASONS IN THE HAWAIIAN ISLANDS.

Avocado, or **Alligator Pears**	June-August.
Bananas	All the year round.
Cherimoyas	November-December.
China Oranges	All the year round.
Cocoa Nuts	All the year round.
Custard Apples	September-October.
Dates	June-October.
Eugenie	June-August.
Figs	Nearly all the year.
Garcinia	May-July.
Grapes	June-October.
Guavas (native)	Nearly all the year.
Guavas (strawberry)	January-December.
Java Plums	July-November.
Limes	All the year round.
Litchie	July-September.
Loquats	July-January.
Mamme Apple	July-November.
Mangoes	June-September.
Mulberries	July-October.
Muskmelons	June-November.
Ohias	June-November.
Oranges	All the year round.
Papaias	All the year round.
Peaches	June-September.
Pine Apples	June-August.
Pomegranates	June-October.
Rose Apples	June-October.
Sapota Pear	June-October.
Sour Sop	Nearly all the year.
Spanish Cherries	May-September.
Strawberries	February-September.
Tamarinds	Nearly all the year.
Vis	June-November.
Water Lemons	July-October.
Water Melons	May-October.
Whampee	July-September.

COFFEE.

COFFEE THE NEW INDUSTRY.

The sugar mills and process of producing the article in different degrees of color for exportation, are described in the "ECHOES OF A KINGDOM;" the machinery required for this purpose is very expensive. Only large investors seem to make fortunes in the sugar market. Coffee is the new industry and product, being extensively cultivated, and bids fair to bring a large revenue to the islands. The coffee planting is mostly in the forest lands, cleared by specified contract labor of Chinese and Japanese. Three years are required before first crop is matured. These same coffee lands are favorable for other plantings and vegetation, and energetic investors can find other sources of income. The islands are especially valuable for coffee plantations at Hawaii, Maui and Molokai. Elevation of land for this purpose is from two hundred to twenty-six hundred feet above the sea level, although in some cases planted near the sea, the cultivation has proved successful.

These islands seem to have within their reach every possibility. There are the highlands and the lowlands; where one species of vegetation may wither and die the other affords all the necessary strength and nourishment for the experimental plant or seed imported by the newly arrived investor. It is possible that as yet only half is revealed, as to the possibilities of vegetation on the islands. Hawaii may well be proud of her resources.

FERNS.

LIST OF HAWAIIAN FERNS.

Kindness of Dr. A. B. Lyons, Former Resident of Hawaii.

Marattia Douglasii	Baker.
Schizaea robusta	Baker.
Gleichenia longissima	Blume.
Gleichenia dicbotana	Hooker.
" Hawaiiensis	Hooker.
Cibotium Menzeesii	Hooker.
" Chamissoi,	Kaulfuss.
" glaucum	Hook. & Arm.
Aceostichum squamosum,	Schwartz.
" Miceadenium	Fee.
" Conforme	Schwartz.
" wawrae	Luerssen.
" reticulatum	Kaulfuss.
" gorgonum	Kaulfuss.
Gymnogramme javanica	Blume.
Vittaria Elongata	Swartz.
Colgpodium Hookeri	Brack.
Pr pseudogrammitis	Gand.
Polypodium Sawoeuse	Baker.
" lineare	Thumberg.
" Spectrum	Kaulfuss.
" Serrulatum	Metten.
" Hsaliliosnum	Brack.
" saementosum	Brack.
" Adenopliorus	Hook. & Arm.
" pellucidum	Kaulfuss.
" hymenoplylloides	Kaulfuss.
" abictiuum	Eaton.
" Tamaiiscinum	Kaulfuss.
" Hillebrandi	Hooker.
Phegopteris polycarpa	Hilleb.
" Kerandreniana	Mann.
" crinalis	Mann.
" Hillebrandi	Hilleb.
" Spinnloas	Hilleb.
" punctata	Hilleb.

Phegopteris unidentata...Mann.
" Sandwicensis....................................Mann.
Aspidium apiifolium...Schk.
" Bogdiae...Eaton.
" Cyatheoides,......................................Kaulfuss.
" caryotideum......................................Wall.
" unitum..Schwartz.
" truncatum...Gandichand.
" globuliferum....................................Mann.
" Filix-mas...Schwartz.
" Hillebrandi..Carruthers.
" aculeatum, vas.........................Beraunii Doell.
" rubigiuosumm..................................Mann.
" latifcous..Brack.
" squamigerum,.....................................Mann.
" Hawaiiense..Hilleb.
" aeistatum...Swartz.
" glabrum..Metten.
Vepheolepis exaltata..Schott.
Cystopluis Douglasii..Hooker.
Sadulia Sreleytiana...Hilleb.
" cyatheoides......................................Kaulfuss.
" pallida..Hook. & Arm.
" squarrosa..Mann.
Doodia media..R. Brown.
" kuntbiana..Gand.
Asplenium Nidus...Linn.
" Trichomaues.....................................Lin.
" veonauthemum................................Lin.
Asplenium uormale..Don.
" fragile..Presl.
" erectum...Boey.
" resectum...Smith.
" contignum..Kaulfuss.
" candatum..Fors.
" nitidulum..Hilleb.
" Kundseuii...Hilleb.
" pseudofalcatum..............................Hilleb.
" Manuii..Hilleb.

Ferns.

Asplenium	Kaulfussii	Schlecht.
"	enatum	Brack.
"	Horridum	Kaulfuss.
"	lobulatum	Metten.
"	spathuliunm	Hook.
"	variaus	Hook. & Grev.
"	Lydgatei	Hilleb.
"	insititium	Brack.
"	bipiunatum	Hilleb.
"	furcatum	Thumb.
"	Adiautum-nigrum	Lin.
Asplenium	acuminatum	Hook & Arm.
"	pulyphyllum	Reeve.
"	pateus	Kaulf.
"	sphenotomum	Hilleb.
"	dissectum	Brack.
"	marginale	Hilleb.
"	Fenzliauum	Luerssen.
"	aeboieum	Wild.
"	sandwiceuse	Hilleb.
"	aeuottii	Baker.
"	sandwichianum	Metten.
"	depaeoides	Brack.
"	aspidioides	Schledet.
"	Baldwini	Hilleb.
Depaeia prolifaa		Hooker.
Lindsaya erecta		Hooker.
"	pumila	Hooker.
"	centifolia	Hilleb.
"	falcata	Hooker.
"	laciniata	Hilleb.
"	Alexandri	Hilleb.
Lindsaya Kundseuii		Hilleb.
"	Maunii	Hilleb.
Odontoloma repeus		Desn.
Miceolepia strigosa		Presl.
"	heita	Kaulf.
"	Jamaiceusis	Fee.
"	tennifolia	Metten.

Ptuis decipilus...Hooker.
" decors..Hooker.
" cutica..Lin.
" irregularis..Kaulf.
" regularis..E. Bailey.
" excelsa...Gandichand.
" aquilina..Lin.
Schizostege Lydgatei.....................................Hilleb.
Pellaca teruifolia...Fee.
Adiantum Capillus-venuis.................................Lin.
Trichesuaues paroulum....................................P——
" intia uaesuale....................Hook. & Grev.
" Dragtoniauum.........................Brack.
" meifolium...............................Bory.
" davallioides.............................Gand.
" crytotheca..............................Hilleb.
Hymeuoplegllum-Baldwini...............................Eaton.
" recusoum...............................Gand.
" lauceolatum........................Hook & Arn.
" obtusum..............................Hook & Arn.
Ophioglossum pendulum...................................Lin.
" nudicaule..............................Lin. fils.
" vulgatum.................................Lin.
" Botrychium sub-bifoliatum...............Brack.

Besides these there are upwards of 90 forms regarded as varieties of some of the above species.

Two genera only are peculiar to the Hawaiian Islands, Sadluia (near Blechuum) with four species, and Schizostege, allied to Ptuis—a simple species.

DR. A. B. LYONS,
Former Resident of Hawaii.

ORGAN RECITAL.

KAUMAKAPILI CHURCH.
OPENING OF THE NEW ORGAN,
SATURDAY EVENING, APRIL 7, 1888,
BY MR. WRAY TAYLOR,
AT 7:45 O'CLOCK.

PROGRAMME.

"HAWAII PONOI."

Kaumakapili March in F	Wray Taylor
Berceuse in A	Delbruck
Evening Prayer	Smart
Fantasia in C. Major	Tours
Carillons de Dunkerque (1780)	Carter-Turpin
Prelude and Fugue in C	Bach
Fantasia Pastorale	Wely
Andante in C	Silas
Flute Concerto	Rink
War March from Athalie	Mendelssohn

"God Save the Queen."
"Star Spangled Banner."
"Hawaii Ponoi."

www.ingramcontent.com/pod-product-compliance
Lightning Source LLC
Chambersburg PA
CBHW030346170426
43202CB00010B/1263